EMMANUEL JOSEPH

The Human Algorithm, Integrating Politics, Society, Psychology, Health, and Business for a Better Future

Copyright © 2025 by Emmanuel Joseph

All rights reserved. No part of this publication may be reproduced, stored or transmitted in any form or by any means, electronic, mechanical, photocopying, recording, scanning, or otherwise without written permission from the publisher. It is illegal to copy this book, post it to a website, or distribute it by any other means without permission.

First edition

This book was professionally typeset on Reedsy.
Find out more at reedsy.com

Contents

1	Chapter 1: The Interwoven Tapestry of Humanity	1
2	Chapter 2: Political Policies and Social Impact	3
3	Chapter 3: The Role of Psychology in Shaping Society	5
4	Chapter 4: Health as a Cornerstone of Prosperity	7
5	Chapter 5: The Business of Building a Better Future	9
6	Chapter 6: Education as a Pillar of Societal Growth	11
7	Chapter 7: The Intersection of Technology and Humanity	13
8	Chapter 8: The Role of Culture in Shaping Societal Values	15
9	Chapter 9: The Economics of Well-being	17
10	Chapter 10: Environmental Sustainability and Human...	19
11	Chapter 11: The Power of Collective Action	21
12	Chapter 12: The Importance of Mental Health	23
13	Chapter 13: The Role of Leadership in Shaping the Future	25
14	Chapter 14: The Impact of Media on Society	27
15	Chapter 15: The Future of Work in a Changing World	29
16	Chapter 16: The Role of Innovation in Driving Progress	31
17	Chapter 17: Building a Better Future Together	33

1

Chapter 1: The Interwoven Tapestry of Humanity

In our rapidly evolving world, understanding the intricate web that connects politics, society, psychology, health, and business is crucial. Each of these domains influences the other, creating a complex algorithm that dictates the trajectory of human progress. From the policies that govern our lives to the societal norms we adhere to, our mental and physical well-being, and the business strategies that shape our economies, everything is interconnected. The first step towards a better future is recognizing and embracing this interdependence. By doing so, we can create more holistic solutions to the challenges we face, paving the way for a more harmonious and prosperous world.

The interplay between these domains is akin to the delicate balance of nature. Just as an ecosystem thrives on the interdependence of its elements, our society flourishes when these domains are in harmony. Politics provides the framework within which society operates, while societal norms and values shape the political landscape. Psychology offers insights into human behavior, informing policies that promote well-being and social cohesion. Health is the bedrock of a thriving society, and businesses drive economic growth and innovation. By recognizing the interconnectedness of these domains, we can develop strategies that leverage their synergies for the collective good.

Moreover, the human algorithm is not static; it evolves with the changing dynamics of our world. As new challenges and opportunities emerge, our understanding of these domains must adapt accordingly. This requires a commitment to continuous learning and collaboration across disciplines. By fostering a culture of interdisciplinary dialogue and innovation, we can address complex issues more effectively and create a more resilient and adaptive society. The human algorithm, therefore, is a dynamic process that requires constant refinement and recalibration to navigate the complexities of our modern world.

Ultimately, the goal is to create a future where politics, society, psychology, health, and business work in concert to enhance human well-being and prosperity. This requires a holistic approach that considers the interplay of these domains and strives for balance and harmony. By embracing the interconnectedness of the human algorithm, we can pave the way for a brighter and more sustainable future for all.

2

Chapter 2: Political Policies and Social Impact

Political decisions have far-reaching consequences on society. Policies around education, healthcare, and the economy determine the quality of life for individuals and communities. A well-crafted policy can uplift marginalized groups, reduce inequalities, and promote social cohesion. Conversely, misguided policies can exacerbate disparities and create social unrest. Therefore, politicians and policymakers must consider the broader social impact of their decisions. By fostering inclusive and equitable policies, we can create a society where everyone has the opportunity to thrive, regardless of their background or circumstances.

One of the key challenges in policy-making is balancing the diverse needs and interests of different groups. This requires a deep understanding of the social fabric and the factors that contribute to inequality and exclusion. Policymakers must engage with communities, listen to their voices, and incorporate their perspectives into the decision-making process. By adopting a participatory approach, we can create policies that are more responsive to the needs of the people they serve and promote social justice.

In addition to addressing immediate social issues, political policies must also consider long-term implications. This involves taking a proactive stance on emerging challenges, such as climate change, technological disruption, and demographic shifts. By anticipating these trends and developing forward-looking policies, we can create a more resilient and adaptable society. Furthermore, policies must be evidence-based, drawing on rigorous research and data to inform decision-making. This requires collaboration between policymakers, researchers, and practitioners to ensure that policies are grounded in reality and have a tangible impact.

Ultimately, the goal of political policies should be to create a society where all individuals have the opportunity to reach their full potential. This requires a commitment to equity, inclusion, and social justice. By fostering a political culture that values these principles, we can create a more cohesive and harmonious society. The human algorithm must prioritize the social impact of political decisions to ensure that they contribute to the collective well-being and progress of humanity.

3

Chapter 3: The Role of Psychology in Shaping Society

Psychology plays a critical role in shaping societal norms and behaviors. Understanding human cognition, emotions, and behavior can inform more effective social policies and interventions. For example, insights from psychology can help address mental health issues, improve educational outcomes, and promote positive social interactions. By integrating psychological principles into policy-making and social programs, we can create environments that support mental well-being and foster healthy, thriving communities. Furthermore, addressing the psychological needs of individuals can lead to more resilient and adaptable societies, better equipped to navigate the complexities of modern life.

One of the key contributions of psychology is the understanding of human motivation and behavior. By exploring the underlying drivers of behavior, we can develop interventions that promote positive change and prevent harmful behaviors. For example, cognitive-behavioral approaches have been effective in treating mental health disorders, while behavioral economics has informed policies that encourage healthy behaviors, such as reducing smoking and promoting physical activity. By leveraging these insights, we can create programs and policies that are more effective in promoting well-being and social cohesion.

Psychology also sheds light on the impact of social and environmental factors on mental health and behavior. For example, social support, community engagement, and positive relationships are critical for mental well-being. Conversely, social isolation, discrimination, and adverse childhood experiences can have detrimental effects on mental health. By addressing these factors, we can create environments that promote mental well-being and reduce the risk of mental health issues. This requires a holistic approach that considers the interplay of individual, social, and environmental factors in shaping mental health and behavior.

In addition to informing social policies, psychology also plays a crucial role in shaping organizational practices and workplace environments. For example, insights from organizational psychology can inform strategies to enhance employee well-being, productivity, and engagement. By creating supportive and inclusive workplaces, organizations can foster a culture of well-being and resilience. Furthermore, addressing mental health in the workplace can lead to more productive and innovative teams, better equipped to navigate the challenges of the modern world.

Ultimately, the role of psychology in shaping society is to promote well-being and social cohesion. By integrating psychological principles into policy-making, social programs, and organizational practices, we can create environments that support mental health and foster positive social interactions. The human algorithm must prioritize the psychological needs of individuals to ensure holistic well-being and resilience in the face of change.

4

Chapter 4: Health as a Cornerstone of Prosperity

Health is fundamental to human well-being and prosperity. A healthy population is more productive, creative, and capable of contributing to societal progress. Public health policies and healthcare systems play a crucial role in ensuring that individuals have access to the care they need. Moreover, addressing social determinants of health, such as education, housing, and income, can significantly improve health outcomes. By prioritizing health in policy-making and investing in comprehensive healthcare systems, we can create a foundation for a more prosperous and equitable future. Health must be viewed not merely as the absence of disease but as a holistic state of physical, mental, and social well-being.

One of the key challenges in public health is addressing health inequalities. Disparities in access to healthcare, quality of care, and health outcomes persist across different populations. These disparities are often rooted in social determinants of health, such as socioeconomic status, education, and housing. By addressing these underlying factors, we can reduce health inequalities and promote health equity. This requires a comprehensive approach that integrates health policies with social and economic policies to create conditions that support health for all individuals.

In addition to addressing health inequalities, public health policies must also consider the broader determinants of health, such as environmental factors and lifestyle behaviors. For example, policies that promote clean air and water, safe and accessible transportation, and healthy food environments can significantly improve health outcomes. Furthermore, promoting healthy behaviors, such as physical activity and healthy eating, can prevent chronic diseases and enhance overall well-being. By adopting a holistic approach to public health, we can create environments that support health and well-being for all individuals.

Healthcare systems also play a critical role in promoting health and well-being. This includes providing access to quality care, preventive services, and health education. Moreover, healthcare systems must be responsive to the changing needs of populations, such as the rise in chronic diseases and aging populations. This requires a shift towards more person-centered and integrated care models that prioritize prevention, early intervention, and chronic disease management. By investing in comprehensive healthcare systems, we can create a foundation for a healthier and more resilient society.

Ultimately, health is a cornerstone of prosperity. By prioritizing health in policy-making and investing in comprehensive healthcare systems, we can create a foundation for a more equitable and prosperous future. The human algorithm must prioritize health to ensure holistic well-being and resilience in the face of change. By viewing health as a holistic state of physical, mental, and social well-being, we can create conditions that support health for all individuals and contribute to the collective prosperity of humanity.

5

Chapter 5: The Business of Building a Better Future

Businesses have a profound impact on society and the environment. Corporate decisions influence employment, economic stability, and ecological sustainability. Therefore, businesses must adopt practices that align with broader societal goals. This includes embracing corporate social responsibility, promoting ethical practices, and investing in sustainable development. By doing so, businesses can drive positive change and contribute to a better future. Furthermore, fostering innovation and entrepreneurship can lead to new solutions for societal challenges. By leveraging their resources and influence, businesses have the potential to be powerful catalysts for social and economic progress.

In today's globalized world, businesses operate within a complex web of stakeholders, including employees, customers, suppliers, communities, and the environment. The decisions made by business leaders have ripple effects that extend far beyond the immediate confines of the company. As such, it is imperative for businesses to consider the broader implications of their actions and strive to create value for all stakeholders. This requires a shift from a narrow focus on short-term profits to a more holistic approach that prioritizes long-term sustainability and social responsibility.

One of the key ways in which businesses can contribute to a better future is by embracing corporate social responsibility (CSR). CSR initiatives can take many forms, from environmental sustainability programs to community development projects and ethical labor practices. By integrating CSR into their core business strategies, companies can enhance their reputation, build stronger relationships with stakeholders, and contribute to the well-being of society. Moreover, CSR can drive innovation by encouraging companies to develop new products and services that address societal needs and challenges.

In addition to CSR, businesses must also prioritize ethical practices and transparency. This includes promoting fair labor practices, ensuring supply chain integrity, and maintaining high standards of corporate governance. By fostering a culture of ethics and accountability, businesses can build trust with stakeholders and create a more just and equitable society. Furthermore, ethical practices can enhance business performance by reducing risks, improving employee morale, and attracting socially conscious consumers.

Ultimately, businesses have the potential to be powerful agents of change. By adopting practices that align with broader societal goals and investing in sustainable development, businesses can drive positive change and contribute to a better future. The human algorithm must recognize the critical role of businesses in shaping society and encourage them to act as responsible and ethical stewards of the planet.

6

Chapter 6: Education as a Pillar of Societal Growth

Education is a cornerstone of societal growth and development. It empowers individuals with knowledge, skills, and critical thinking abilities, enabling them to contribute meaningfully to society. Access to quality education is essential for reducing inequalities and fostering social mobility. By investing in education, we can cultivate a more informed, engaged, and capable citizenry. Furthermore, education systems must evolve to meet the demands of a changing world. This includes integrating technology, promoting lifelong learning, and fostering creativity and innovation. By prioritizing education, we can create a foundation for sustained societal progress and prosperity.

One of the key challenges in education is ensuring equitable access for all individuals, regardless of their socioeconomic background, gender, or geographic location. Disparities in access to education can perpetuate cycles of poverty and inequality, limiting opportunities for social mobility. To address these disparities, governments and organizations must invest in infrastructure, resources, and programs that support inclusive and equitable education. This includes providing scholarships, financial aid, and support services for marginalized and underserved communities.

In addition to promoting equity, education systems must also evolve to meet the demands of a rapidly changing world. Technological advancements, globalization, and shifting labor markets are transforming the skills and knowledge required for success. Education must therefore prioritize critical thinking, problem-solving, and adaptability, as well as technical skills and digital literacy. By integrating technology into the curriculum and promoting innovative teaching methods, we can prepare students for the challenges and opportunities of the future.

Furthermore, education should not be limited to formal schooling but should encompass lifelong learning. In a world where change is constant, individuals must continually update their skills and knowledge to remain relevant and competitive. This requires creating opportunities for adult education, vocational training, and professional development. By fostering a culture of lifelong learning, we can ensure that individuals have the tools and resources to navigate the complexities of the modern world.

Ultimately, education is a pillar of societal growth and development. By investing in equitable and inclusive education systems, we can empower individuals to reach their full potential and contribute meaningfully to society. The human algorithm must prioritize education to create a foundation for sustained progress and prosperity.

7

Chapter 7: The Intersection of Technology and Humanity

Technology is transforming every aspect of our lives, from how we communicate to how we work and learn. While technological advancements offer immense opportunities, they also pose significant challenges. It is crucial to navigate the ethical implications of technology and ensure that it serves the greater good. This includes addressing issues such as data privacy, digital divide, and the impact of automation on employment. By fostering responsible innovation and inclusive access to technology, we can harness its potential to improve lives and create a more equitable and just society. The human algorithm must evolve to incorporate technological advancements while preserving our core values and principles.

One of the most significant impacts of technology is its ability to connect people across distances and create new forms of communication and collaboration. Social media, video conferencing, and other digital platforms have transformed how we interact and share information. However, these technologies also raise concerns about data privacy, misinformation, and digital addiction. It is essential to develop policies and practices that protect individuals' privacy and promote responsible use of technology. This includes educating users about digital literacy and ethical online behavior.

The digital divide is another critical challenge that must be addressed to ensure equitable access to technology. Disparities in access to digital resources and infrastructure can exacerbate existing inequalities and limit opportunities for marginalized communities. Governments and organizations must invest in digital infrastructure, provide affordable access to technology, and promote digital literacy programs. By bridging the digital divide, we can create a more inclusive and connected society where everyone has the opportunity to benefit from technological advancements.

Automation and artificial intelligence (AI) are transforming the labor market, with significant implications for employment and economic stability. While these technologies have the potential to enhance productivity and create new job opportunities, they also pose the risk of job displacement and economic disruption. It is crucial to develop policies that support workers in transitioning to new roles and industries, such as retraining and reskilling programs. By fostering a culture of lifelong learning and adaptability, we can ensure that individuals are prepared to navigate the changing world of work.

Ultimately, the intersection of technology and humanity presents both opportunities and challenges. By fostering responsible innovation and inclusive access to technology, we can harness its potential to improve lives and create a more equitable and just society. The human algorithm must prioritize ethical considerations and social responsibility to ensure that technology serves the greater good and enhances human well-being.

8

Chapter 8: The Role of Culture in Shaping Societal Values

Culture is a powerful force that shapes societal values, norms, and behaviors. It influences how we perceive and interact with the world around us. Cultural diversity enriches our communities and fosters creativity and innovation. By embracing cultural pluralism and promoting intercultural understanding, we can build more inclusive and cohesive societies. This requires a commitment to preserving cultural heritage while fostering dialogue and collaboration across different cultural groups. By valuing and respecting cultural diversity, we can create a more harmonious and resilient global community.

One of the key ways in which culture shapes societal values is through the transmission of traditions, beliefs, and practices. These cultural elements provide a sense of identity and belonging, helping individuals navigate their social environments. However, cultural norms can also perpetuate inequalities and exclusion. It is essential to critically examine cultural practices and promote values that support equality, justice, and human rights. By fostering a culture of inclusion and respect, we can create environments where all individuals feel valued and empowered.

Cultural diversity is a source of strength and resilience for societies. It fosters creativity and innovation by bringing together diverse perspectives and experiences. By embracing cultural pluralism, we can promote social cohesion and build more inclusive communities. This requires creating spaces for intercultural dialogue and collaboration, as well as promoting policies that support cultural diversity. Governments, organizations, and communities must work together to create environments that value and respect cultural differences while fostering a sense of shared identity and purpose.

In addition to promoting intercultural understanding, it is essential to preserve and celebrate cultural heritage. This includes protecting cultural sites, traditions, and languages, as well as supporting cultural expressions such as art, music, and literature. By valuing and preserving cultural heritage, we can strengthen our connections to the past and create a sense of continuity and belonging. Furthermore, cultural heritage can serve as a source of inspiration and innovation, enriching our communities and fostering a sense of pride and identity.

Ultimately, culture plays a crucial role in shaping societal values and fostering social cohesion. By embracing cultural diversity and promoting intercultural understanding, we can create more inclusive and harmonious societies. The human algorithm must prioritize the role of culture in shaping societal values and promote a culture of inclusion, respect, and collaboration.

9

Chapter 9: The Economics of Well-being

Economic policies and systems play a crucial role in shaping the well-being of individuals and societies. Traditional economic measures, such as GDP, often fail to capture the true quality of life. Therefore, it is essential to adopt a more holistic approach to economics that prioritizes well-being and sustainability. This includes addressing income inequality, promoting fair labor practices, and ensuring access to essential services such as healthcare and education. By prioritizing well-being in economic decision-making, we can create a more equitable and prosperous society. The human algorithm must evolve to integrate economic policies that promote both prosperity and social justice.

One of the key limitations of traditional economic measures is their focus on material wealth and productivity. While these indicators are important, they do not fully capture the well-being of individuals and communities. Well-being encompasses a broad range of factors, including physical and mental health, social connections, and environmental sustainability. To truly assess the well-being of a society, we must consider these factors alongside economic performance. This requires developing new metrics that capture the multi-dimensional nature of well-being and using them to inform policy decisions.

Addressing income inequality is a critical component of promoting well-being. Economic disparities can have far-reaching consequences, including reduced access to essential services, lower life expectancy, and increased social unrest. To address these issues, policymakers must implement progressive taxation, social safety nets, and policies that promote fair labor practices. By reducing income inequality, we can create a more inclusive and cohesive society where everyone has the opportunity to thrive.

Promoting fair labor practices is another essential aspect of the economics of well-being. This includes ensuring safe and healthy working conditions, fair wages, and opportunities for career advancement. By protecting workers' rights and promoting decent work, we can enhance the quality of life for individuals and families. Furthermore, investing in education and training programs can help workers adapt to the changing labor market and access new opportunities. By prioritizing fair labor practices, we can create a more just and equitable economy that benefits all members of society.

Ultimately, the economics of well-being requires a shift from a narrow focus on material wealth to a more holistic approach that prioritizes the quality of life. By integrating well-being and sustainability into economic decision-making, we can create a more equitable and prosperous society. The human algorithm must evolve to embrace this holistic approach and prioritize policies that promote both prosperity and social justice.

10

Chapter 10: Environmental Sustainability and Human Flourishing

The health of our planet is intrinsically linked to the well-being of humanity. Environmental sustainability is essential for ensuring a livable future for generations to come. This requires a commitment to reducing carbon emissions, conserving natural resources, and protecting biodiversity. By adopting sustainable practices in every aspect of our lives, from energy consumption to waste management, we can mitigate the impact of climate change and preserve the planet's ecosystems. Furthermore, fostering a sense of environmental stewardship and responsibility can lead to more sustainable and mindful communities. The human algorithm must prioritize environmental sustainability to ensure the long-term flourishing of humanity.

One of the key challenges in promoting environmental sustainability is addressing the overconsumption of natural resources. Our current consumption patterns are unsustainable and place immense pressure on the planet's ecosystems. To address this issue, we must adopt more sustainable consumption practices, such as reducing waste, recycling, and choosing environmentally friendly products. Additionally, governments and businesses must implement policies and practices that promote resource conservation and reduce environmental impact. By adopting a more sustainable approach to resource use, we can protect the planet's ecosystems and ensure a livable future for generations to come.

Reducing carbon emissions is another critical component of environmental sustainability. Climate change poses a significant threat to the health and well-being of humanity, with far-reaching consequences for ecosystems, economies, and communities. To mitigate the impact of climate change, we must transition to renewable energy sources, improve energy efficiency, and reduce greenhouse gas emissions. This requires a concerted effort from governments, businesses, and individuals to adopt sustainable practices and invest in clean energy technologies. By reducing carbon emissions, we can mitigate the effects of climate change and protect the planet for future generations.

Protecting biodiversity is also essential for environmental sustainability. Biodiversity provides essential ecosystem services, such as pollination, water purification, and climate regulation. The loss of biodiversity can have devastating consequences for ecosystems and human well-being. To protect biodiversity, we must conserve natural habitats, protect endangered species, and promote sustainable land and water use practices. Additionally, fostering a sense of environmental stewardship and responsibility can encourage individuals and communities to take action to protect the planet's biodiversity. By prioritizing biodiversity conservation, we can ensure the long-term health and resilience of ecosystems and the well-being of humanity.

Ultimately, environmental sustainability is essential for the long-term flourishing of humanity. By adopting sustainable practices, reducing carbon emissions, and protecting biodiversity, we can mitigate the impact of climate change and preserve the planet's ecosystems. The human algorithm must prioritize environmental sustainability to ensure a livable future for generations to come.

11

Chapter 11: The Power of Collective Action

Collective action is a powerful force for driving social change and addressing global challenges. By coming together and working towards common goals, individuals and communities can create meaningful and lasting impact. This includes advocating for social justice, promoting human rights, and addressing issues such as poverty and inequality. Grassroots movements, community organizations, and global coalitions all play a vital role in mobilizing collective action and fostering a sense of shared responsibility. By harnessing the power of collective action, we can build a more just and equitable world. The human algorithm must recognize the importance of collaboration and solidarity in creating positive change.

One of the key strengths of collective action is its ability to amplify the voices of marginalized and underrepresented communities. Grassroots movements and community organizations provide platforms for individuals to advocate for their rights and push for social change. By working together, individuals can challenge systemic injustices and demand accountability from those in power. Collective action can also foster a sense of empowerment and solidarity, encouraging individuals to take an active role in shaping their communities and advocating for positive change.

Collective action is also essential for addressing global challenges that transcend national borders, such as climate change, human rights, and public health. Global coalitions and international organizations play a crucial role in coordinating efforts and mobilizing resources to address these issues. By fostering collaboration and partnerships across sectors and countries, we can develop comprehensive and effective solutions to global challenges. Additionally, collective action can promote a sense of shared responsibility and global citizenship, encouraging individuals and communities to work together for the common good.

In addition to advocating for social change, collective action can also drive innovation and creativity. By bringing together diverse perspectives and experiences, collective action can generate new ideas and solutions to complex problems. Collaborative initiatives, such as community-driven development projects and social enterprises, can leverage the strengths and resources of different stakeholders to create positive impact. Furthermore, collective action can foster a culture of collaboration and mutual support, encouraging individuals and organizations to work together towards common goals.

Ultimately, the power of collective action lies in its ability to bring individuals and communities together to create meaningful and lasting change. By advocating for social justice, promoting human rights, and addressing global challenges, collective action can build a more just and equitable world. The human algorithm must recognize the importance of collaboration and solidarity in driving positive change and foster a culture of collective action.

12

Chapter 12: The Importance of Mental Health

Mental health is a critical component of overall well-being. It affects how we think, feel, and interact with others. Addressing mental health issues is essential for creating a healthy and thriving society. This includes promoting mental health awareness, providing access to mental health services, and reducing stigma. By integrating mental health into public health policies and social programs, we can support individuals in achieving their full potential. Furthermore, fostering environments that promote mental well-being, such as supportive workplaces and communities, can lead to more resilient and adaptable societies. The human algorithm must prioritize mental health to ensure holistic well-being.

One of the key challenges in addressing mental health is reducing the stigma associated with mental illness. Stigma can prevent individuals from seeking help and support, leading to worsening mental health outcomes. To combat stigma, we must promote mental health awareness and education, encouraging open conversations about mental health and challenging misconceptions. By normalizing discussions about mental health, we can create a more supportive and inclusive environment where individuals feel empowered to seek help and support.

Access to mental health services is another critical aspect of promoting mental well-being. Many individuals face barriers to accessing mental health care, such as cost, lack of availability, and social stigma. To address these barriers, we must invest in mental health infrastructure and services, ensuring that individuals have access to affordable and high-quality care. This includes expanding mental health services in primary care settings, integrating mental health into public health policies, and providing support for community-based mental health programs. By improving access to mental health services, we can support individuals in achieving their full potential and promoting overall well-being.

Creating environments that promote mental well-being is also essential for fostering resilient and adaptable societies. This includes supportive workplaces that prioritize employee well-being, schools that promote positive mental health, and communities that foster social connections and support. By creating environments that support mental well-being, we can reduce the risk of mental health issues and promote positive mental health outcomes. This requires a holistic approach that considers the social, economic, and environmental factors that influence mental health.

Ultimately, mental health is a critical component of overall well-being. By promoting mental health awareness, improving access to mental health services, and creating supportive environments, we can support individuals in achieving their full potential and fostering resilient and adaptable societies. The human algorithm must prioritize mental health to ensure holistic well-being and create a healthier and more thriving society.

13

Chapter 13: The Role of Leadership in Shaping the Future

Leadership plays a crucial role in shaping the trajectory of societies and organizations. Effective leaders inspire and mobilize individuals towards common goals, fostering a sense of purpose and direction. This includes promoting ethical leadership, encouraging innovation, and addressing complex challenges with empathy and integrity. By cultivating visionary and inclusive leaders, we can drive positive change and create a better future. Furthermore, leadership is not limited to formal positions of power; it can be demonstrated at every level of society. By empowering individuals to take on leadership roles, we can harness the collective potential of humanity.

One of the key qualities of effective leadership is the ability to inspire and motivate others. Visionary leaders can articulate a clear and compelling vision for the future, encouraging individuals to work towards common goals. This requires effective communication, emotional intelligence, and the ability to build trust and rapport with others. By inspiring and mobilizing individuals, leaders can create a sense of purpose and direction, fostering a collective effort towards positive change.

Ethical leadership is also essential for building trust and integrity within organizations and societies. Ethical leaders prioritize transparency, accountability, and fairness, ensuring that their decisions and actions align with their values and principles. By promoting ethical leadership, we can create a culture of trust and integrity, where individuals feel valued and respected. Furthermore, ethical leaders can navigate complex challenges with empathy and integrity, fostering a sense of moral responsibility and social justice.

Innovation is another critical aspect of effective leadership. Visionary leaders encourage creativity and innovation, fostering a culture of continuous learning and improvement. This includes promoting a growth mindset, encouraging risk-taking, and supporting individuals in developing new ideas and solutions. By fostering a culture of innovation, leaders can drive positive change and create a better future. Additionally, innovative leaders can adapt to changing circumstances and navigate uncertainty, ensuring the long-term success and resilience of their organizations and societies.

Ultimately, leadership plays a crucial role in shaping the future. By cultivating visionary, inclusive, and ethical leaders, we can drive positive change and create a better future for all. The human algorithm must prioritize the role of leadership in shaping the trajectory of societies and organizations, empowering individuals to take on leadership roles and harness the collective potential of humanity.

14

Chapter 14: The Impact of Media on Society

The media plays a powerful role in shaping public opinion and influencing societal norms and behaviors. It has the potential to inform, educate, and inspire individuals. However, it can also perpetuate misinformation, bias, and divisiveness. Therefore, it is essential to promote responsible and ethical journalism that prioritizes truth, accuracy, and inclusivity. By fostering media literacy and critical thinking skills, we can empower individuals to navigate the complex media landscape and make informed decisions. The human algorithm must recognize the impact of media on society and strive to promote a more informed and engaged citizenry.

One of the key challenges in the media landscape is the prevalence of misinformation and fake news. Misinformation can have far-reaching consequences, influencing public opinion, exacerbating social divisions, and undermining trust in institutions. To combat misinformation, it is essential to promote responsible and ethical journalism that prioritizes truth and accuracy. This includes fact-checking, transparent sourcing, and accountability in reporting. By fostering a culture of responsible journalism, we can ensure that individuals have access to accurate and reliable information.

Media literacy is another critical aspect of navigating the media landscape. Media literacy involves the ability to critically evaluate and interpret media messages, recognizing bias, and distinguishing between credible and unreliable sources. By promoting media literacy education, we can empower individuals to navigate the complex media landscape and make informed decisions. This includes teaching critical thinking skills, encouraging skepticism, and promoting awareness of the impact of media on society. By fostering media literacy, we can create a more informed and engaged citizenry.

The media also has the potential to promote inclusivity and diversity. By representing diverse perspectives and voices, the media can foster social cohesion and promote understanding and empathy. This requires a commitment to inclusive and equitable representation, ensuring that marginalized and underrepresented communities have a platform to share their stories and experiences. By promoting diversity and inclusivity in the media, we can create a more just and equitable society.

Ultimately, the media plays a powerful role in shaping public opinion and influencing societal norms and behaviors. By promoting responsible and ethical journalism, fostering media literacy, and encouraging diversity and inclusivity, we can create a more informed and engaged citizenry. The human algorithm must recognize the impact of media on society and strive to promote a media landscape that supports truth, accuracy, and inclusivity.

15

Chapter 15: The Future of Work in a Changing World

The nature of work is undergoing significant transformations due to technological advancements, globalization, and shifting societal values. This presents both opportunities and challenges. It is essential to adapt to these changes by promoting lifelong learning, fostering innovation, and ensuring fair labor practices. By embracing new ways of working, such as remote work and the gig economy, we can create more flexible and inclusive work environments. Furthermore, addressing issues such as job displacement and income inequality is crucial for creating a future of work that benefits everyone. The human algorithm must evolve to navigate the changing world of work and ensure that it contributes to human flourishing.

One of the key drivers of change in the world of work is technological advancements. Automation, artificial intelligence, and digital technologies are transforming how we work, creating new opportunities for efficiency and innovation. However, these technologies also pose the risk of job displacement and economic disruption. To navigate these changes, it is essential to invest in education and training programs that prepare individuals for the jobs of the future. This includes promoting digital literacy, supporting reskilling and upskilling initiatives, and fostering a culture of lifelong learning.

By preparing individuals for the changing world of work, we can ensure that they have the skills and knowledge to thrive in a rapidly evolving labor market.

Globalization is another key factor shaping the future of work. Globalization has expanded access to markets and created new opportunities for economic growth. However, it has also led to increased competition and economic inequality. To address these challenges, it is essential to promote fair labor practices and ensure that the benefits of globalization are equitably distributed. This includes protecting workers' rights, promoting fair wages, and supporting inclusive economic policies. By fostering a more equitable global economy, we can create a future of work that benefits everyone.

Shifting societal values are also influencing the future of work. There is a growing emphasis on work-life balance, flexibility, and meaningful work. To meet these changing expectations, organizations must adopt more flexible and inclusive work practices. This includes promoting remote work, supporting the gig economy, and creating inclusive and supportive work environments. By embracing new ways of working, organizations can attract and retain talent, foster innovation, and create a more engaged and motivated workforce.

Ultimately, the future of work is shaped by a complex interplay of technological advancements, globalization, and societal values. By adapting to these changes, promoting lifelong learning, and ensuring fair labor practices, we can create a future of work that benefits everyone. The human algorithm must evolve to navigate the changing world of work and ensure that it contributes to human flourishing.

16

Chapter 16: The Role of Innovation in Driving Progress

Innovation is a key driver of progress and human development. It has the potential to address some of the most pressing challenges facing humanity, from healthcare to environmental sustainability. By fostering a culture of innovation and supporting research and development, we can create new solutions and opportunities for growth. This includes investing in science and technology, promoting entrepreneurship, and encouraging collaboration across sectors. The human algorithm must prioritize innovation to drive progress and create a better future. Furthermore, ensuring that the benefits of innovation are accessible to all is essential for promoting equity and social justice.

One of the key ways in which innovation drives progress is through the development of new technologies and solutions. Breakthroughs in fields such as medicine, renewable energy, and information technology have the potential to transform our lives and address critical challenges. By investing in research and development, we can accelerate the pace of innovation and bring new solutions to market. This requires a commitment to funding scientific research, supporting innovation ecosystems, and promoting policies that encourage experimentation and risk-taking.

Promoting entrepreneurship is another critical aspect of fostering innovation. Entrepreneurs play a vital role in bringing new ideas to life and driving economic growth. By supporting entrepreneurship, we can create a fertile ground for innovation and empower individuals to pursue their creative ideas. This includes providing access to capital, mentorship, and resources for startup ventures, as well as creating an enabling regulatory environment. By fostering a culture of entrepreneurship, we can unlock the potential of individuals and drive positive change.

Collaboration across sectors is also essential for driving innovation. Many of the most significant innovations emerge at the intersection of different fields and disciplines. By promoting interdisciplinary collaboration and partnerships, we can bring together diverse perspectives and expertise to tackle complex challenges. This includes fostering collaboration between academia, industry, government, and civil society. By breaking down silos and promoting cross-sector collaboration, we can create a more dynamic and innovative ecosystem.

Ultimately, innovation is a key driver of progress and human development. By fostering a culture of innovation, promoting entrepreneurship, and encouraging collaboration, we can create new solutions and opportunities for growth. The human algorithm must prioritize innovation to drive progress and create a better future for all.

17

Chapter 17: Building a Better Future Together

As we navigate the complexities of the modern world, it is essential to recognize that the future is a collective endeavor. The challenges we face are multifaceted and interconnected, requiring a holistic and collaborative approach. By integrating politics, society, psychology, health, and business, we can create a more harmonious and prosperous world. This requires a commitment to equity, justice, and sustainability, as well as a recognition of our shared humanity. The human algorithm must evolve to embrace these principles and prioritize the well-being of all individuals and communities.

One of the key elements of building a better future is fostering a sense of shared responsibility and global citizenship. We must recognize that our actions have far-reaching consequences and that we are all interconnected. By promoting a sense of global citizenship, we can encourage individuals to take an active role in addressing global challenges and advocating for positive change. This includes promoting education and awareness about global issues, fostering empathy and understanding, and encouraging individuals to take action in their communities and beyond.

Equity and justice are also essential components of a better future. We must strive to create a world where all individuals have the opportunity to thrive, regardless of their background or circumstances. This requires addressing systemic inequalities, promoting social justice, and ensuring that the benefits of progress are equitably distributed. By prioritizing equity and justice, we can create a more inclusive and cohesive society where everyone has the opportunity to reach their full potential.

Sustainability is another critical element of building a better future. We must recognize that the health of our planet is intrinsically linked to the well-being of humanity. By adopting sustainable practices and policies, we can mitigate the impact of climate change, protect natural resources, and ensure a livable future for generations to come. This requires a commitment to environmental stewardship and responsibility, as well as a recognition of the interconnectedness of social, economic, and environmental systems.

Ultimately, building a better future requires a collective effort. By integrating politics, society, psychology, health, and business, we can create a more harmonious and prosperous world. The human algorithm must evolve to embrace these principles and prioritize the well-being of all individuals and communities. Together, we can navigate the complexities of the modern world and create a brighter future for all.

And there you have it, the concluding chapters of "The Human Algorithm: Integrating Politics, Society, Psychology, Health, and Business for a Better Future." This completes the exploration of how these interconnected domains shape our world and how we can collectively work towards a better future. If you have any questions or need further adjustments, feel free to let me know!

The Human Algorithm: Integrating Politics, Society, Psychology, Health, and Business for a Better Future

In an increasingly interconnected world, understanding the intricate web that links politics, society, psychology, health, and business is vital for fostering a more harmonious and prosperous future. "The Human Algorithm" delves into the multifaceted relationships among these domains, revealing how they shape our lives and influence human progress.

This enlightening book takes readers on a journey through the interwoven tapestry of humanity, exploring how political decisions impact social structures, how psychological insights inform societal norms, and how health serves as the cornerstone of prosperity. It examines the transformative power of businesses in driving positive change and the pivotal role of education in societal growth.

"The Human Algorithm" also addresses the profound impact of technology on humanity, the significance of cultural diversity, and the importance of prioritizing well-being in economic policies. It underscores the urgency of environmental sustainability and the power of collective action in creating a just and equitable world.

Throughout its 17 chapters, this book presents a holistic approach to understanding the complex interplay of these domains, offering insights and strategies for integrating them to enhance human well-being. By fostering a culture of innovation, promoting ethical leadership, and embracing global citizenship, "The Human Algorithm" provides a blueprint for building a better future together.

Join the journey to uncover the connections that bind us and discover how we can collectively navigate the challenges of the modern world to create a brighter future for all.

www.ingramcontent.com/pod-product-compliance
Lightning Source LLC
LaVergne TN
LVHW020459080526
838202LV00057B/6038